SHAPEDBYSCRIPTURE

And God Said to Abraham

GENESIS
12-27

ALEX VARUGHESE

The Foundry Publishing
PO Box 419527
Kansas City, MO 64141
thefoundrypublishing.com

978-0-8341-3819-3

Printed in the
United States of America

Cover Design: J.R. Caines
Interior Design: J.R. Caines
Layout: Sharon Page

10 9 8 7 6 5 4 3 2 1

Contents

Introduction

THE *SHAPED BY SCRIPTURE* SERIES

The first step of an organized study of the Bible is the selection of a biblical book, which isn't always an easy task. Often people pick a book they are already familiar with, or books they think will be easy to understand, or books that, according to popular opinion, seem to have more relevance to Christians today than other books of the Bible. However, it is important to recognize the truth that God's Word is not limited to just a few books. All the biblical books, both individually and collectively, communicate God's Word to us. As Paul affirms in 2 Timothy 3:16, "All Scripture is God-breathed and is useful for teaching, rebuking, correcting and training in righteousness." We interpret the term "God-breathed" to mean inspired by God. If Christians are going to take 2 Timothy 3:16 seriously, then we should all set the goal of encountering God's Word as communicated through all sixty-six books of the Bible. New Christians or those with little to no prior knowledge of the Bible might find it best to start with a New Testament book like 1 John, James, or the Gospel of John.

By picking up this volume, you have chosen to study the book of Genesis. You've made a great choice because this first book of the Bible lays a foundation for the rest of the story of God. Because the goal of this series is to illustrate an appropriate method of studying the Bible, instead of a comprehensive study of the entire book, our study will be limited to a few select passages in Genesis. In the first volume, we focused on seven stories taken from chapters 1–11. We will take up another set of seven stories from chapters 12–27 in this second volume of our study of Genesis.

How This Study Works

This Bible study is intended for a period of seven weeks. We have chosen a specific passage for each week's study. This study can be done individually or with a small group.

For individual study, we recommend a five-day study each week, following the guidelines given below:

1	On the first day of the study, read the relevant passage several times until you become fully familiar with the verses, words, and phrases.
2	On the second day, we will review the setting and organization of the passage.
3	On the third day, we will observe some of the realities portrayed in the passage.
4	On the fourth day, we will investigate the relationship of the individual passage to the larger story of God in the Bible.
5	On the fifth day, we will reflect on the function of the story as we hear it today, the invitation it extends to us, and our response to God, who speaks through God's Word.

If this Bible study is done as a group activity, we recommend that members of the group meet together on the sixth day to share and discuss what they have learned from God's Word and how it has transformed their lives.

You may want to have a study Bible to give you additional insights as we work through the book of Genesis. Another helpful resource is *Discovering the Old Testament*, available from The Foundry Publishing.

Literary Forms in the Bible

There are several literary forms represented throughout the Bible. The divinely inspired writers used various techniques to communicate God's Word to their ancient audiences. The major literary forms (also known as genres) of the Bible are:

- narratives
- laws
- history
- Wisdom literature (in the form of dialogues and proverbial statements)
- poetry (consisting of poems of praise, lament, trust in God, and more)
- prophecy
- discourses
- parables
- miracle stories
- letters (also known as epistles)
- exhortations
- apocalyptic writings

Within each of these forms, one may find subgenres. Each volume in the *Shaped by Scripture* series will briefly overview the genres found in the book of the Bible that is the subject of that study.

When biblical writers utilized a particular literary form, they intended for it to have a specific effect on their audience. This concept can be understood by examining genres that are familiar to us in our contemporary setting. For example, novels that are comedies inspire good and happy feelings in their readers; tragedies, on the other hand, are meant to induce sorrow. What is true of the intended effect of literary forms in contemporary literature is also true of literary forms found in the Bible.

THE BOOK OF GENESIS

The message of the biblical books, though it originates with God, comes to us through individuals whom God inspired to communicate his word to humanity. They fulfilled their task by utilizing their literary skill as speakers and writers of God's message. This message came to these individuals in particular circumstances in the history of God's people—the Israelites in the Old Testament period, and the early Christian church in the first century AD. In addition, biblical books communicate certain clearly developed understandings about God, humanity, sin, judgment, salvation, human hope, and more. Bible studies should be done with an awareness of the theological themes in a particular book. So, prior to our engagement with the actual text of Genesis, we shall briefly summarize what we know about the authorship of Genesis, literary forms found in the book, the historical setting of the book and that of its writing, the literary structure of the book, and its major theological themes.

Who Wrote Genesis?

The book of Genesis belongs to a collection of five biblical books that are known as the Pentateuch in the Jewish tradition. They can also be called the Five Books, the Five Scrolls, the Law, or the Torah. In addition to Genesis, the collection includes Exodus, Leviticus, Numbers, and Deuteronomy. Some scholars hold to the ancient Jewish and Christian view of these books as the work of Moses, but others think it is possible that they have multiple authors. Genesis is a collection of Israel's oral traditions about creation and the beginning of human history; and about Abraham, Isaac, and Jacob—the three foremost ancestors of the people group that later came to be called Israel. Though the authorship of Genesis and many other biblical books is frequently debated among Christians, we believe in the integrity of the biblical books as we find them in the Bible today.

Literary Form

The book of Genesis is considered narrative. It is written mostly in prose and is made up of stories. In chapters 1–11, the narrative focus is on creation and humanity as a whole. From chapters 12–50, we read the stories of the family of Abraham, Isaac, and Jacob. These stories deal with events that have taken place in the history of this family and the interactions of its various members with those within their family as well as outsiders. As a result of this familial focus, most of the stories in chapters 12–50 belong to a subcategory called *family stories*—in which a prominent individual plays a key role as the main character. In addition to the stories, Genesis also contains genealogical lists (in chapters 5, 10, 25, 36, and 46) that indicate the ancestries of various groups of people who once lived in the ancient world.

Entering the Story

Stories in Genesis (and in the rest of the Bible) are intended to draw readers into the various scenes portrayed in them. In other words, biblical stories are never meant to remain ancient stories, and readers are never meant to be detached from them. Reading a Genesis story is like being in a stadium and watching an exciting game. Very rarely do we see people at sporting events remain in the bleachers, unemotional and detached from the game. Most sports fans see themselves as part of the team, cheering victories and yelling at the players when they fail to execute the game plan. Likewise, the writers of Genesis invite us to enter into the story and become part of it. When we do, we soon discover that most of the narratives portray realities very much like those that exist in our world today. We find in the biblical characters reflections of our imperfect relationships, our doubts, our mistrust of God or others, our pride, our self-reliance, our violence, our family quarrels and rivalries, our cheating and deception, our hatred or mistreatment of others who are not like us. Even the few individuals we find in Genesis who demonstrate great personal integrity have character flaws.

Entering into a Genesis story and seeing ourselves and our own world through the lens of that story does not mean that the intended effect of the story has been accomplished entirely. Most of the Genesis stories relate to some crisis. In Genesis, we often find God entering into the midst of human crisis and addressing the characters in order to give instructions for resolving the crisis. When God's involvement is not directly reported in a particular story, we usually find it in preceding stories about the same character. Just like the people we know in real life, some of the characters in Genesis respond to God's voice and resolve their crisis; others do not.

The stories in Genesis accomplish their intended effect when readers respond to the invitation, or the challenge, they encounter inside the stories. The characters we meet in Genesis and their interactions with a faithful God motivate us to think of or imagine the alternative to our own crisis-ridden lives. How would a Genesis story change if the characters listened to God and took action to promote the healing of broken relationships and the well-being of others around them? How would our world look today if we did the same?

Genesis stories invite us to enter into and embrace the world God intended for us to live when God brought forth creation. We find the perfect model for such existence in the life of Jesus in the New Testament Gospels. By following the example of Jesus, and through our faith in him, we become God's new creation in the world. When we do this, and become what God originally created us to be, then we can say that the Genesis stories have had their intended effect. Personal transformation is the final effect intended by the stories in Genesis. In this way of reading and studying, we see the stories in Genesis extending beyond their ancient context and becoming God's living Word to us today!

This is the method of reading and studying the Bible we will follow in this book. We admit that this method is somewhat different from many popular Bible study materials and methods found in the marketplace today. Most of them seek to lay out theological, moral, ethical principles that can be derived from the stories and then applied to our life situations today. Without denying the merit of these types of resources, we suggest instead that life transformation, instead of life application, should be the goal of a Bible study—and transformation is, therefore, our goal in the *Shaped by Scripture* series.

Historical Context

We deal with two important and separate but related issues when we investigate the date and the historical context of Genesis (this is true of an investigation of all the biblical books). First, we examine the time and the particular context (historical, political, cultural, social, and religious) in which the stories of Genesis took place. Second, we examine the date and the context in which the book was actually composed by its editors/compilers. Both of these issues are important for us to consider. The former helps us to place specific stories in their particular setting, which is critical to our understanding of the realities portrayed in the stories. The latter helps us to discover how later generations would have heard and understood these stories.

Context of the Events in Genesis

Unfortunately, we cannot place the events in Genesis chapters 1–11 in a specific historical period because the events reported in them come from a period long before the documenting of history and civilization by humans began. We can only say that these events belong to the earliest period of human history and reflect the widely held beliefs of the Israelites about the origin of the world and humanity. They also set the context for the stories of Abraham, Isaac, and Jacob in chapters 12–50.

The stories in chapters 4–11 are filled with gaps. Though they are put together in a seamless fashion, we think the writers preserved only major incidents that changed the course of human history. For example, the writers cover the creation of the world through approximately 2000 BC in only eleven chapters. However, it takes them thirty-nine chapters (12–50) to tell the stories of Abraham, Isaac, and Jacob—the three great ancestors of the people who would later become the Israelites. This difference clearly suggests that the primary goal of the writers was to tell their own story.

Most scholars agree that these stories belong to the period of the Amorite civilization in Mesopotamia, Syria, and Palestine (roughly 2000–1700 BC). Scholars also believe that Abraham was part of a migratory movement of the Amorites from Mesopotamia into the Syria-Canaan region (see Genesis 11:27–32). The ancestors of the Israelites lived as seminomadic people who pitched their tents in places where they found pasture for their flock. They were not part of an organized religious group. They worshiped God by setting up altars and offering sacrifices. The head of the household carried out the priestly tasks.

Though Abraham himself once belonged to the polytheistic religion of the Amorites, his encounter with God led him to his belief in one true God, whom he called "Most High, Creator of heaven and earth" (Genesis 14:22). Scholars consider Abraham to be the founder of monotheism—belief in one God. Abraham, his son Isaac, and his grandson Jacob worshiped God by setting up altars in the places where God appeared to them during their travels.

Other than these sketchy details, we do not know much about the setting of the stories found in chapters 12–50.

Context of the Writing of Genesis

Most scholars believe that Genesis in its present form was written in the sixth century BC, when the Jewish people were living in exile in Babylon, after the Babylonians conquered Judah and brought an end to their political freedom in 586 BC. The exile threatened the future of the Jewish people and their identity as the covenant people of God in the world.

It is possible that the writer(s) of Genesis collected and compiled the oral stories from the past and put them together in written form with two goals in mind: (1) to provide the Jews in Babylon and future generations a foundational understanding of Israel's God as the creator and sustainer of the world; (2) to give the Jewish community a clear understanding of their identity and mission in the world—which is that, though they are exiles, living away from the land God promised to their ancestors, they continue to be God's people. They belong to the family of Abraham, and they are a people with a mission to the world. The mission God gave to Abraham to be an instrument of God's blessing to all peoples on earth is their same, continued mission.

Investigating the context in which the books of the Bible were written is important when we hear God's Word today. Although the circumstances may differ, God's Word speaks today in our own life situations. So, although the details are different, we are able to experience Scripture in fresh and new ways. As we listen to the story of God in the Bible, we can experience God's Word as God's "living word" today.

Literary Structure

The fifty chapters in Genesis are organized under two major sections: chapters 1–11 contain several stories that deal with humanity as a whole. This section begins with two stories about God's creation of the world and humankind (chapters 1–2), followed by the story of humankind's first sin and the consequences that followed (chapter 3). The story of chapter 4 shows that violence has become a way of life in the world. Chapter 5 is a genealogical list that traces the ancestry of Noah, who is the main character in the story of the flood and who represents a new beginning for humanity in chapters 6–9. Chapter 10 is another genealogy that identifies the descendants of the three sons of Noah. Chapter 11 begins with another story of human rebellion against God and the consequence that followed, and ends with another genealogy that traces the ancestral line from Noah (through his son Shem) down to Terah and his better-known son Abraham (still known as Abram at this point).

Genesis chapters 12–50 contain the stories of Abraham, Isaac, and Jacob. Abraham stories are found from 12:1–25:18. Though Isaac's family is introduced in 25:19–34, we find him as the main hero only in the stories in chapter 26. The rest of the stories in Genesis (chapters 27–50) center on Jacob, who becomes the father of the twelve tribes of Israel. Though Joseph stories dominate chapters 37–50, Jacob remains in the background and plays a key role in the journey of the family from Canaan to Egypt, where they settle after the deaths of Jacob and Joseph. Thus, the stories in chapters 37–50 serve to set the scene for the book of Exodus, which begins with the story of Israel's centuries-long enslavement in Egypt.

Major Theological Themes

Genesis, though mostly filled with stories of families and individuals, contains many significant theological themes. The fact that Genesis begins with the account of God's creation of the world and everything in it leads us to surmise that the creation theme has a central place in the book. The following list shows how the various other themes in Genesis are connected to the creation theme.

Creation testifies to God's nature as a relational God. Through God's creation activities, God entered into a faithful relationship with God's creation (1:1–2:4).

Blessing is a fundamental way God relates to God's creation. God's blessing is the source of the growth and well-being of creation (1:22, 28; 2:3).

The God-given mission of human beings is to be God's image in the world. We do this through faithful relationship with God and with the rest of creation (1:26–28).

We are designated caretakers of creation. The authority God grants to humans is that of shepherds, not of despotic, exploitive, destructive rulers (1:26–28).

God created Sabbath rest. God's rest on the seventh day of creation models a work-rest rhythm for creation's existence (2:2–3).

Living in obedience to God is critical to faithful relationship with God (2:15–17).

Human beings failed to be God's image in the world. This failure resulted in a disruption of our relationship with God and with the rest of creation (3:1–24).

Sin through disobedience and rebellion against God became a destructive and pervasive reality in the world. God's judgment was the inevitable consequence of human sin (4:1-7:24).

In the midst of the judgment of the flood, God remained gracious and created a new beginning for humanity through Noah and his family (6:9–9:17).

Noah's descendants resisted God's mandate to spread over the entire earth. As a result, God's judgment came upon them (11:1–9; see also 1:28; 9:1).

God entered into a special covenant relationship with Abraham. God promised to bless Abraham with numerous descendants and a land as their inheritance from God (12:1–3; 15:1–21; 17:1–27).

God's promise of blessing to Abraham and his family (and all other human families) is an extension of God's blessing on creation (see 1:22, 28).

God promised to bless "all peoples on earth" through Abraham (12:3). The mission of the covenant family was to be an instrument of God's blessing to others.

Isaac and Jacob became the recipients of God's covenant promises to Abraham (26:1–6; 28:10–22).

The future of Abraham and his family was shaped not only by the promises of God but also by their obedience to God (several stories in chapters 12–50 illustrate the obedient response of Abraham, Isaac, and Jacob to God's commands).

God remained faithful to Joseph, a member of the covenant family, and surrounded him with God's presence during his trouble-filled days in Egypt (39:1–23).

GENESIS 12:1–9

Genesis 12 marks the beginning of the second major segment of the story of Genesis. Here we find the beginning of the story of Israel. This story begins with God's command and promises to Abraham, the great ancestor of the people of Israel. The story of Abraham (chapters 12–25) is followed by the stories of Abraham's son Isaac (chapter 26), Isaac's son Jacob (chapters 27–36), and Jacob's twelve sons (chapters 37–50). Compared with the rather fragmentary stories of chapters 1–11, the details in Genesis 12–27 and 28–50 indicate that the author's primary goal was to tell the story of Israel's ancestors. Chapters 1–11 provide the universal setting of the stories of chapters 12–50. The story of Abraham in 12:1–9 is set in the larger context of God's scattering of the descendants of Noah following the Tower of Babel incident (11:1–9).

WEEK 1, DAY 1

Listen to the story in Genesis 12:1–9 by reading it aloud several times until you become familiar with its verses, words, and phrases. Enjoy the experience of imagining the story in your mind, picturing each event as it unfolds.

WEEK 1, DAY 2

The Setting

In Genesis 11:27–32 we find the historical setting of one of the most important events in the second part of Genesis: Abraham's encounter with God. Scholars place the story of Abraham in the early part of the second millennium—a time when the Amorites, a Semitic people group, controlled most of Mesopotamia and Syria-Palestine (2000–1700 B.C.). Verse 27 identifies Abraham as one of the three sons of Terah, who was a descendant of Shem, who in turn was one of the three sons of Noah. Verse 31 tells us that Abraham came from Ur, an urban center in the southern part of Mesopotamia. Additionally, he belonged to the Amorite/Aramean ethnic group (see Deuteronomy 26:5); the Hebrews may have lived as a subculture within this group (see Genesis 14:13).

The writer may mention Terah and his family's migration from Ur (11:31) to show that they were part of the scattered people of Babel (11:9). Eventually, Terah's family (which includes Abraham and Sarah*) decided to set out for Canaan, about 1,200 miles from Ur. However, once they made it to Haran (an approximate halfway point on the journey to Canaan), they decided to settle there instead. Genesis 11 ends with Terah's death in Haran (verse 32). We can infer that, after his father's death, Abraham assumed responsibility for the family and its future. The family established strong roots in Haran—Abraham refers to this area as his "country" and his "native land" in Genesis 24:4, 7.

Genesis 11:27–32 tells us very little about Abraham, except that his wife, Sarah, was barren. However, it is possible to see the reference to Sarah's barrenness as another context for the story of 12:1–9—Abraham and Sarah were not only a part of the scattered human family, but because of their childlessness, they were also living without any hope for their future. In that sense, God's words to Abraham in 12:1–3 were meant to give him hope for the future.

Keeping in mind the overview above, as well as the larger story of God's creation, human sin, and human resistance to God's creational purpose (see Genesis 1–11), we will now dive into Genesis 12:1–9—the story of Abraham's encounter with God.

---

*Abraham and Sarah are called Abram and Sarai until their names change in Genesis 17. For simplicity's sake, we will call them only Abraham and Sarah throughout this study.

The Plot

Now let's look carefully at how the writer organizes the story of 12:1–9—the plot will become clear as we examine the various parts of this story. Based on the transitions we notice in these verses, we can break 12:1–9 into five smaller paragraphs. Let's examine each of those five paragraphs one at a time. **Beneath each grouping of verses, write the primary idea or theme they communicate (follow the pattern provided for 12:1, 2–3. and 4–5).**

1. Genesis 12:1

God commands Abraham to leave his country and go to the land that God will show him.

2. Genesis 12:2–3

God makes several promises to Abraham.

3. Genesis 12:4–5

Abraham obeys God and leaves Haran with his family and possessions and arrives in the land of Canaan.

4. Genesis 12:6–7

5. Genesis 12:8–9

WEEK 1, DAY 3

What's Happening in the Story?

As we notice certain circumstances in the story, we will begin to see how they are similar to or different from the realities of our world. The story will become the lens through which we see the world in which we live today. In our study today, you may encounter words and/or phrases that are unfamiliar to you. Some of the particular words and translation choices for them have been explained in more detail in the **Word Study Notes**. If you are interested in even more help or detail, you can supplement this study with a Bible dictionary or other Bible study resource.

1. Genesis 12:1

Abraham's story begins with words from the LORD.[1] God begins his speech by commanding Abraham to "go"[2] from his country and family relations—to separate himself from everyone he knows, from the less intimate ("country") to the more intimate ("father's household"). This emphasis on separation indicates that God is aware of the difficulty Abraham will experience in obeying. What's more, God doesn't give Abraham a specific destination for his journey; he simply calls it "the land I will show you."[3] In order to obey, then, Abraham must step out in faith—he must follow God's guidance and trust God to reveal the destination.

2. Genesis 12:2–3

God makes a series of promises to Abraham, each beginning with "I will," which expresses God's personal commitment to carry out his promises. God's promises begin with his commitment to make the childless Abraham "into a great nation."[1] His descendants will increase in number and become a nation among other nations in the world. God also promises to "bless"[2] Abraham and make his "name great."[3] Moreover, God commands Abraham not just to receive blessings but also to be a blessing to others.[4]

WORD STUDY NOTES #1

[1] The Bible has not recorded a speech from God to humans since his speech to Noah (see Genesis 9:1–17). For that reason, this divine speech to Abraham marks an important turning point in God's relationship with humankind.

[2] The command "go" in Hebrew is a command to separate oneself from familiar surroundings.

[3] See a similar phrase, "on a mountain I will show you," in Genesis 22:2.]

WORD STUDY NOTES #2

[1] God's blessings promised to Abraham in this story are an extension of God's creational blessing in Genesis 1.

[2] The Hebrew root *brk* or *barak* (meaning "to bless") is found five times in these verses, which indicates the importance of blessing in God's promises to Abraham. In the Old Testament, *brk* often conveys the idea of material and physical prosperity and fruitfulness.

[3] A great name means fame and renown in the world. This promise indicates that God alone can make individuals and nations great.

[4] "You will be a blessing" in Hebrew is a command, indicated by the imperative verb form.

God makes it clear that Abraham is not the only one who will receive blessings; he promises to bless all who bless Abraham. God also promises to "curse" those who curse Abraham. God thus promises to deal with the people in the land where Abraham is going according to the way they treat Abraham.

God ends his promises with the announcement that, through Abraham, he will bless "all peoples on earth." This indicates that God's ultimate purpose in blessing Abraham is to extend his blessings and reach others in the world. In proclaiming this, God assigns Abraham the role of a mediator—he will be the person God will work through in his plan to bless the world.

Practice the above pattern to write a short description of the world portrayed in verses 4–9.

WORD STUDY NOTES #3

[1] Abraham became the guardian of Lot after Terah's death in Haran (see 11:27-31).

[2] The reference to Canaan implies that it was "the land" God had promised to show Abraham.

3. Genesis 12:4–5[1, 2]

WORD STUDY NOTES #4

[1] Abraham and his family would have traveled nearly 500 miles to arrive at Shechem from Haran.

[2] "Canaanites" here is an umbrella term for the native inhabitants of Canaan, most likely made up of several ethnic groups.

4. Genesis 12:6–7[1, 2]

5. Genesis 12:8–9[1, 2]

____

____

____

____

____

____

____

WORD STUDY NOTES #5

[1] The phrase "called on the name of the LORD" in the Bible indicates the worship of God.

[2] Negev, which means "dry land," extends from the southern part of the Judean hills all the way down to Kadesh. Scholars consider the Negev to be the area where Abraham lived his nomadic life in Canaan.

Discoveries

Let's summarize some of our discoveries from Genesis 12:1–9.

1. God commanded Abraham to leave everything he knew behind and embark on a journey under his direction.
2. God did not give Abraham a destination for his journey; the fact that Abraham obeyed indicates that he trusted God for guidance.
3. God followed his command to Abraham by promising to bless him with descendants and give him honor and reputation in the world.
4. God commanded Abraham to be a blessing to others in the world.
5. God promised to bless those who honored Abraham, and to withhold his providential care from those who mistreated him.
6. God promised to bless all peoples on earth through Abraham.
7. Abraham obeyed God's command without questioning or hesitation.
8. Abraham built an altar as a sign of his trust in God and worshiped him at the place where God appeared to him.
9. Abraham continued his travels to the desert region called Negev.

WEEK 1, DAY 4

The Call of Abraham and the Story of God

If you have a study Bible, you will notice that there are marginal references that point to other biblical texts. You may want to look up some of those Scriptures to help you understand how the whole story of God ties together!

When we read a biblical text, it is important to ask how it relates to the rest of the Bible. Genesis 12:1–9 outlines the first of the four major events through which God brought Israel, his covenant people, into existence. The other three events are as follows: 1) God delivers Israel from slavery in Egypt and makes a covenant with them at Mount Sinai; 2) God provides for Israel in the wilderness for forty years; and 3) God brings Israel into the land of Canaan. Abraham's obedience and faith in this story remain a source of inspiration to all who trace their physical or spiritual heritage back to him.

Abraham's story continues with more stories of God appearing to him and issuing commands, and Abraham faithfully responding to God. These encounters include God's covenant with Abraham (chapter 17) and God's command for Abraham to offer Isaac as a burnt offering (chapter 22). Abraham's relationship with God was continued by his son Isaac, and later, by Isaac's son Jacob. God entered into a covenant relationship with Abraham, Isaac, and Jacob's descendants and called them to be mediators of his blessings to the world (Exodus 19:5–6). The covenant people's failure to do so forms the context for God sending his son Jesus into the world. It is important to note that both Matthew and Luke identify Jesus, who God used to fulfill his salvation plan, as a physical descendant of Abraham (Matthew 1:1–17; Luke 3:23–34).

The biblical story is filled with echoes of Genesis 12:1–9—God's promises to Abraham, and Abraham's faith in God.

Let's consider some biblical passages that are directly or indirectly related to this story or its themes. **In the space provided below, write a short summary of how various elements of this story are reflected in each passage.**

1. Genesis 13:14–17

____

____

2. Genesis 15:2–5

3. 2 Samuel 7:9

4. Psalm 72:17

5. Acts 7:1–5

6. Hebrews 11:8–9

WEEK 1, DAY 5

Genesis and Our World Today

When we enter into the intriguing narrative of Genesis 12:1–9, the story becomes the lens through which we see ourselves, our world, and God's action in our world today.

1. What does the Genesis story of God calling Abraham say to us about ourselves, our world, and God's action in our world today?

God continues to call us to follow him and obey his directions for our lives. God's call to follow him may come to us in the midst of our hopelessness and life apart from him. God may speak to us when we least expect to hear his voice.

Describe below what prevents us from hearing God's voice today.

2. How would you react to an unexpected call from God to leave everything behind and embark on a journey with him?

3. What are the things that are most difficult for us to be separated from, if God would ask us to leave everything behind and follow his directions for our lives?

4. In what ways have you been blessed by God?

5. In what ways have you been a blessing to others?

Invitation and Response

God's Word always invites a response. Think about the way the story of God calling Abraham speaks to us today. How does the story invite us to respond?

God is aware of the difficulty Abraham will experience in obeying God's command. Abraham must follow God's guidance and trust God to reveal the destination.

GENESIS 13

The story of Lot and his separation from Abraham is related to the stories in chapters 14, 18–19. These stories provide a glimpse into the tribal relationship between Abraham's descendants and the people groups who lived to the south and east of the promised land, particularly the Ammonites and the Moabites. The purpose of these stories is to show Abraham's conduct toward those who lived outside of the covenant promises. In chapter 13, Abraham behaves in an exemplary way—he is a model of generosity and faithfulness in his relationship with Lot. In chapter 14, he goes to war and rescues Lot and his possessions, along with the goods of Sodom and Gomorrah, from a coalition of eastern kings. In chapter 18, he intercedes on behalf of the inhabitants of Sodom and attempts to persuade God to spare the city from destruction. Chapter 19 links the Ammonites and Moabites, the historic enemies of Israel, to an incestuous relationship between Lot and his two daughters.

WEEK 2, DAY 1

Listen to the story in Genesis 13 by reading it aloud several times until you become familiar with its verses, words, and phrases. Enjoy the experience of imagining the story in your mind, picturing each event as it unfolds.

WEEK 2, DAY 2

The Setting

The two stories of Abraham in chapter 12 provide the immediate setting for the story of 13:1–18. Abraham was introduced in chapter 11 as a descendant of Shem (one of the three sons of Noah), and as a member of the human community that was scattered after the Tower of Babel incident. The first story shows his radical obedience to God's command to leave his relations in Haran and travel to an unknown destination (12:1–9). Along with this command, God promises to give Abraham descendants, bless him, make his name great, and bless all peoples on earth through him. Abraham arrives in Canaan under God's direction, and there, he builds altars and worships God at the places where he camps.

The second story focuses on Abraham's scheme to get rich at his wife's expense. A famine in Canaan prompts Abraham to go to Egypt with his wife and stay there for a while (12:10–20). As they approach Egypt, Abraham asks Sarah to tell the Egyptians that she is his sister—he is afraid that if they realize she is his wife, they'll kill him. He hopes that he'll be treated well because of Sarah.

When Abraham and Sarah enter Egypt, Pharaoh's officials bring Sarah to the palace to be Pharaoh's wife. And sure enough, Pharaoh treats Abraham well because of Sarah; he rewards him with sheep, cattle, donkeys, camels, and servants. However, God afflicts Pharaoh's household with disease, which Pharaoh quickly recognizes as a divine punishment for taking Sarah as his wife. Pharaoh confronts Abraham, exposes his lie, and returns Sarah to him with the command to leave Egypt. So Abraham returns to Canaan a wealthy man, with possessions he acquired in Egypt through falsehood.

We will now approach Genesis 13:1–18, keeping in mind the overview above. In chapter 12, Abraham exemplifies total trust in God's promises, yet also relies on his own shrewdness to survive in Egypt. In the story of chapter 13, Abraham behaves much like the faithful and trusting Abraham in 12:1–9. He also seeks the welfare of others, in contrast to his self-serving behavior in 12:10–20. As we explore Genesis 13:1–18, we also remember that it is set in the larger context established in Genesis 1–11: God's creational plan for humankind, and human sin and resistance to God.

The Plot

Now let's look carefully at how the writer organizes the story of 13:1–18—the plot will become clear as we examine the various parts of this story. Based on the transitions we notice in these verses, we can divide 13:1–18 into five smaller paragraphs.

Let's examine each of those five paragraphs one at a time. **Beneath each grouping of verses, write the primary idea or theme they communicate (follow the pattern provided for 13:1–4, 5–7, and 8–9).**

1. Genesis 13:1–4

Abraham returns to Canaan from Egypt a wealthy man. He travels until he arrives at Bethel, where he previously camped and worshiped God.

2. Genesis 13:5–7

Abraham and Lot's shepherds quarrel.

3. Genesis 13:8–9

Abraham makes a proposal to settle the quarrel.

4. Genesis 13:10–13

5. Genesis 13:14–18

WEEK 2, DAY 3

What's Happening in the Story?

As we notice certain circumstances in the story, we will begin to see how they are similar to or different from the realities of our world. The story will become the lens through which we see the world in which we live today. In our study today, you may encounter words and/or phrases that are unfamiliar to you. Some of the particular words and translation choices for them have been explained in more detail in the **Word Study Notes**. If you are interested in even more help or detail, you can supplement this study with a Bible dictionary or other Bible study resource.

1. Genesis 13:1–4

Abraham returns to Canaan from Egypt with his wife, Sarah, his nephew Lot, and all the possessions he accumulated in Egypt,[1] which includes livestock, silver, and gold.[2] They arrive in the Negev, the southern part of Canaan, and travel north from there until they reach Bethel, the place where Abraham previously camped and worshiped God. Abraham's goal in returning to Bethel was to worship God and thereby renew his relationship with him.

WORD STUDY NOTES #1

[1] While the writer makes no moral judgment about Abraham's conduct or the way he acquired his wealth, Pharaoh's accusation in 12:18–19 makes Abraham's deception clear.

[2] Precious metals would have given a nomadic shepherd like Abraham tremendous economic security, as well as the means to purchase servants and material goods.

2. Genesis 13:5–7

Lot, who has his own flocks and herds and tents, is part of Abraham's nomadic family group—probably because of their close relationship. But because of the scarcity of grazing areas and the increase of their possessions, the two families find it difficult to live together. The quarrel between their herders may center on land and water resources.[1] The writer indicates that the local inhabitants, the Canaanites and Perizzites, also depend on the land's scarce resources.[2]

WORD STUDY NOTES #2

[1] There is nothing unusual about this quarrel since quarreling among nomadic groups over pastures and wells was common in the ancient world (see Genesis 21:22–34; 26:12–33).

[2] We do not know anything about the Perizzites; Genesis 15:19 lists them among the inhabitants of Canaan before the arrival of the Israelites in the land.

3. Genesis 13:8–9

Though this quarrel is not between Abraham and Lot, Abraham takes the initiative to settle the conflict before it affects their relationship. Though God has promised the land to Abraham, and though Abraham has privileges as the elder in the family, he lets Lot choose the area he prefers for his herds and flocks. In doing so, Abraham seeks to separate peacefully from Lot and his family.

Practice the above pattern to write a short description of the world portrayed in verses 10-18.

4. Genesis 13:10–13[1, 2, 3]

____

____

____

____

____

____

5. Genesis 13:14–18[1, 2]

____

____

____

____

____

____

Discoveries

Let's summarize our discoveries from Genesis 13.

1. Abraham returned to Canaan with the wealth he gained in Egypt by lying about Sarah.
2. Abraham traveled to Bethel and worshiped God at the place where he had previously worshiped.

WORD STUDY NOTES #4

[1] "The garden of the LORD" refers to the garden of Eden. This comparison conveys the beauty and richness of the land as well as its potential as a place of temptation.

[2] "The land of Egypt" here is most likely the Nile delta region, known for its rich soil, agricultural productivity, and abundance of food (see Genesis 12:10–20).

[3] The phrase "sinning greatly against the LORD" recalls the offense of Noah's generation (Genesis 6:11–13); it also anticipates God's judgment on the people of Sodom.

WORD STUDY NOTES #5

[1] The "dust" imagery conveys an idea of the unimaginable increase of Abraham's descendants.

[2] In telling Abraham to "walk through the length and breadth of the land," God is instructing him to symbolically take possession of the land for himself and his descendants.

3. Scarcity of resources sparked a quarrel between Abraham's and Lot's herders.
4. Abraham, the elder in the family with power and privileges, offered Lot the first choice of land for his flocks.
5. Lot chose a beautiful and seemingly prosperous place for himself without discernment.
6. God gave Abraham and his descendants the entire land of Canaan as a gift forever.
7. God told Abraham to travel the land, perhaps to symbolically accept God's gift to him and his descendants.
8. Abraham traveled to Hebron, made it his home, and worshiped God there.

WEEK 2, DAY 4

The Story of Abraham and Lot and the Story of God

When we read a biblical text, it is important to ask how it relates to the rest of the Bible. This story does not appear elsewhere in the Bible; it is, however, connected to the stories of Lot in Genesis 14 and the story of the destruction of Sodom and Gomorrah in Genesis 18–19. It is also the earliest biblical example we have of someone seeking peace instead of pursuing the path of conflict—and for that reason, Abraham's behavior in this story is a model for all who seek to do the same. In this story, Abraham establishes the pattern for proper brotherly relationships, which is an important theme in the Bible. By contrasting Abraham's conduct with Lot's, the passage also depicts two ways of life: the way of righteousness that leads to blessing, and the way of wickedness that leads to destruction. The contrast between these two lifestyles is an important theme in Israel's wisdom literature in the psalms and proverbs.

Let's consider some biblical passages that are directly or indirectly related to this story or its themes. **In the space provided below, write a short summary of how various elements of this story are reflected in each passage.**

1. Genesis 12:10–20

In chapter 12, Abraham deceives Pharaoh in an attempt to survive and gain wealth. Chapter 13, however, presents Abraham as a remarkably changed person who does not seek his own benefit but is ready to give up his rights and privileges for peace and for the benefit of others.

2. Genesis 14:1–24

Even after Lot chooses the best part of the land for himself and separates from Abraham, Abraham continues to act as Lot's guardian and protector. When Abraham hears that a coalition of eastern kings has captured Lot, he and his men pursue the captors, rescue Lot and his people, and bring them back to Sodom.

3. Genesis 14:13 and 35:27

4. Genesis 18:16–33

5. Genesis 19:1–29

6. Genesis 26:19–22

7. Genesis 28:14

8. Deuteronomy 34:1–4

9. Proverbs 15:18 and 20:3

10. Matthew 5:9 and 6:33

WEEK 2, DAY 5

Genesis and Our World Today

When we enter into the narrative of Genesis 13, the story becomes the lens through which we see ourselves, our world, and God's action in our world today.

1. What does the story of Abraham and Lot say to us about ourselves, our world, and God's action in our world today?

Like Abraham, we often find ourselves living in two worlds—our self-seeking and self-serving world, and the world of faith and trust in God (see the two contrasting portraits of Abraham in Genesis 12:10–20 and 13:1–18). We also live in the world of God's grace and providential care, even when our faith is weak and our actions betray our trust in ourselves (see 12:10–13:2). Scarcity of resources is often a cause of conflict in our homes and even our churches. We live in a world where greed and profit margins drive economic decisions.

Follow the above example to answer the following:

2. How do conflicts over land and resources often end in our world?

3. How do we handle conflicts over resources in our homes and churches?

4. How does Abraham's example of yielding his rights and privileges to resolve a conflict compare with our own attempts to resolve conflicts in our relationships today?

5. How does Lot's decision to claim the fertile plain of the Jordan compare with the decisions we make today? (Keep in mind the statements about Sodom in 13:10, 13).

6. Abraham's generosity to Lot is the outward expression of his trust in God's promises. What motivates us to be gracious and generous in our relationships?

7. This story begins and ends with Abraham's worship, which indicates that his relationship with God shapes the way he relates to others. What role does worship play in our relationships today?

Invitation and Response

God's Word always invites a response. Think about the way the story of Abraham and Lot speaks to us today. How does the story invite us to respond?

Abraham is a model of generosity and faithfulness in his relationship with Lot.

GENESIS 15

This week's story has special significance to both Jewish and Christian traditions. In the Jewish tradition it is known as "the covenant between the pieces" because of the covenant-making ritual in Genesis 15:7–21. In the New Testament, Paul refers to Abraham's example in 15:6 to argue the case for justification by faith (see Galatians 3).

This chapter presents a new kind of encounter between God and Abraham. Up until now their interactions have followed a particular pattern: God speaks, and Abraham listens and obeys (12:1–4; 13:14–18). But here, for the first time, Abraham dialogues with God. In response to God's command, he also performs a ritual that involves cutting the bodies of certain animals in half (a custom practiced by some ancient Near Eastern cultures during covenant-making ceremonies). The Hebrew expression for instituting a covenant— "*cutting* a covenant"—reflects this practice. Jeremiah 34:17–20 helps us understand the warning inherent in this ritual: the cutting of the animals' bodies symbolizes the fate of the person who would violate the terms of the covenant. In Genesis 15, God makes the covenant and promises Canaan to Abraham and his descendants. In making this promise, God guarantees its fulfillment by invoking the animals' fate upon himself if he fails.

The story has two scenes: verses 1–6, and verses 7–21. The first scene begins with a speech from the Lord in the night (15:1, 5); the second scene also begins with the Lord's speech and takes place in the evening (15:12, 17). In the first speech, the Lord promises Abraham descendants (15:1, 15); in the second, God promises him land (15:18–21). It is not clear if the second scene immediately follows the first or if they are two separate events, but either way, their arrangement communicates continuity.

WEEK 3, DAY 1

Listen to the story in Genesis 15 by reading it aloud several times until you become familiar with its verses, words, and phrases. Enjoy the experience of imagining the story in your mind, picturing each event as it unfolds.

WEEK 3, DAY 2

The Setting

Our story begins with the phrase, "After this," which may refer to the story of Abraham's rescue of Lot in chapter 14, or perhaps to all the events reported in chapters 12–14. Abraham was seventy-five years old when he left Haran after receiving God's promise of land and descendants. We do not know how many years have passed since Abraham first received the promise of descendants; however, the story reflects Abraham's anxiety over the delay in its fulfillment. The next story (chapter 16) reports the birth of Ishmael when Abraham is eighty-six years old; it is likely that the events in chapter 15 take place shortly before Sarah gives Hagar to Abraham.

This story also reveals its Amorite cultural context: an Amorite couple without children had the option of legally adopting a slave so they could have an heir. Additionally, the ritual of cutting an animal's body in half was a part of covenant-making ceremonies in ancient Amorite culture.

The Plot

Now let's look carefully at how the writer organizes the story of 15:1–21—the plot will become clear when we examine the various parts of this story. Based on the transitions we notice in these verses, we can divide 15:1–21 into five smaller paragraphs of verses. Let's examine each of those five paragraphs one at a time. **Beneath each grouping of verses, write the primary idea or theme they communicate (follow the pattern provided for 15:1–6 and 7–9).**

1. Genesis 15:1–6

God responds to Abraham's complaint about being childless by promising him countless descendants.

2. Genesis 15:7–9

After promising to give him Canaan, God asks Abraham to gather certain animals.

3. Genesis 15:10–11

4. Genesis 15:12–16

5. Genesis 15:17–21

WEEK 3, DAY 3

What's Happening in the Story?

As we notice certain circumstances in the story, we will begin to see how they are similar to or different from the realities of our world. The story will become the lens through which we see the world in which we live today. In our study today, you may encounter words and/or phrases that are unfamiliar to you. Some of the particular words and translation choices for them have been explained in more detail in the **Word Study Notes**. If you are interested in even more help or detail, you can supplement this study with a Bible dictionary or other Bible study resource.

1. Genesis 15:1–6

God appears to Abraham in a vision and assures him of his presence[1] and continued protection. God also promises Abraham a great reward. Abraham responds by addressing God as "Sovereign Lord." At the same time, he expresses frustration that, even after God's promise of descendants, he remains childless ("What can you give me since I remain childless?"). This question implies that any further reward is meaningless as long as Abraham has no heir. Furthermore, Abraham is concerned that a servant in his household, Eliezer of Damascus, will be his heir.[2] God responds to Abraham by alleviating his fear; Abraham's own son will be his heir. God confirms this promise by showing him the stars in the sky and promising him not just one son but a multitude of descendants, innumerable as the stars in the sky.[3] Abraham trusts God to fulfill his promise, and God declares[4] Abraham to be righteous—that is, he stands in right relationship with God.

2. Genesis 15:7–11

God speaks to Abraham again and identifies himself as the Lord[1] who brought Abraham out of Ur of the Chaldeans.[2] God reveals to Abraham that he led him out of Ur to give him the land of Canaan. Abraham responds by seeking assurance that he will indeed possess the land. God, in turn, answers with a command to gather a heifer, goat, ram,[3] dove, and pigeon.

WORD STUDY NOTES #1

[1] "Do not be afraid" (or, "fear not") is an announcement of salvation and assurance of God's presence found in a number of places in the Bible.

[2] Following the custom of their day, Abraham and Sarah, as a childless couple, appear to be planning to designate Eliezer to be their heir.

[3] God made the stars (along with the sun and the moon) to be reliable sources of light in the sky. God shows Abraham the stars not as some sort of sign but as a confirmation of the reliability of the promise and the certainty of its fulfillment.

[4] The Hebrew word for "credited" here is the same word used for the approval Israel's priests will later give to proper offerings.

WORD STUDY NOTES #2

[1] This is the first instance of God's self-introduction ("I am the Lord") in the Old Testament. However, according to Exodus 6:2–3, God did not disclose God's name to anyone until he spoke to Moses.

[2] Ur was a prominent center of culture and civilization in third-millennium southern Mesopotamia; it reached its zenith in the early part of the second millennium BC. The Chaldeans were a ruling class who came to prominence in the 7th–6th century BC. The writer here identifies

Abraham likely understands the purpose of this command because, without being prompted, he cuts the animals in two (except the birds) and arranges the halves of each animal across from one another in parallel rows. Abraham drives away birds of prey that come down on the carcasses, probably because he knows that a covenant-making ritual is about to take place.

Practice the above pattern to write a short summary description of the world or reality that is portrayed in verses 12–21.

3. Genesis 15:12–15[1, 2, 3, 4, 5, 6, 7]

4. Genesis 15:17–21[1, 2]

the ancient city with its later influential rulers.

[3] We do not know why God specifically asks for three-year-old animals. These animals would have been fully grown and thus very valuable to Abraham.

WORD STUDY NOTES #3

[1] "Deep sleep" is used to refer to an abnormally heavy sleep that prevents a person from observing God's work (see Genesis 2:21).

[2] "Darkness" here is the mysterious arena of the Lord's work; this text also characterizes darkness as awe-inspiring.

[3] "Four hundred years" here is not a precise number; Exodus 12:40 mentions Israel's life in Egypt for 430 years (see also Galatians 3:17; but see Acts 7:6 for 400 years).

[4] "Great possessions" recalls Abraham's coming out of Egypt with great wealth (12:14–13:2) and anticipates Israel's plundering of the Egyptians (Exodus 12:35–36).

[5] We do not know the precise length of the "fourth generation." If generation means a life cycle, then its length could vary from 120 years (Genesis 6:3) to 100 years (Isaiah 65:20) to 70–80 years (Psalm 90:10).

[6] "The Amorites" here represents the inhabitants of the promised land (the Canaanites).

[7] The phrase "the sin of the Amorites has not reached its full measure" is difficult to interpret. It seems to convey the idea that it takes time for sins to reach their full effects.

WORD STUDY NOTES #4

[1] The smoking firepot and blazing torch symbolize the appearance of God, who initiated the covenant with Abraham. Fire and smoke are common elements in Old Testament theophany narratives (see Exodus 19:16–19; 20:18). ("Theophany" means God appearing to humans.)

[2] Again, the phrase "made a covenant" here can be literally translated from Hebrew as "cut a covenant," referring to the cutting of animal bodies during the covenant ritual.

Discoveries

Let's summarize some of our discoveries from Genesis 15.

1. God appeared to Abraham, assured him of his presence and protection, and promised him a great reward.
2. Abraham acknowledged God's total lordship over his life.
3. God declared Abraham as a righteous person because he believed God's promise.
4. God told Abraham that he brought him out of his native land to give him the land of Canaan.
5. Abraham brought the animals God requested and prepared them for a covenant-making ritual.
6. In a deep sleep, engulfed by thick darkness, Abraham experienced the awe-inspiring presence of God.
7. Though he had not yet fulfilled his promise to give Abraham descendants, God spoke about his future actions in their history.
8. A smoking firepot and blazing torch passed between the pieces of the animals, symbolizing the institution of God's covenant with Abraham.

WEEK 3, DAY 4

The Story of the Covenant and the Story of God

When we read a biblical text, it is important to ask how it relates to the rest of the Bible. In this text, God's covenant with Abraham and his promise to give Canaan to his descendants are major aspects of Israel's faith. Abraham's trust in God's promises and God crediting his faith as righteousness are crucial precedents for the Christian doctrine of justification by faith.

Let's consider some of the biblical passages that directly relate to the different aspects of the story of Genesis 15:1–21. **In the space provided below, write a short summary of how the passages below reflect the concerns of Genesis 15.**

1. Read Genesis 15:1; 26:24; 46:3; Deuteronomy 1:21; Joshua 8:1; Isaiah 41:10; Luke 1:30 and Acts 18:9. What do all these texts have in common?

2. Genesis 22:15–18

3. Exodus 23:20–30

4. Jeremiah 34:18–19

5. Romans 4:1–3

6. Romans 4:20–24

7. Romans 5:1–2

8. James 2:21–24

WEEK 3, DAY 5

Genesis and Our World Today

When we enter into the intriguing narrative of Genesis 15, the story becomes the lens through which we see ourselves, our world, and God's action in our world today.

1. What does the story of God's covenant with Abraham say to us about ourselves, our world, and God's actions in our lives today?

Today we hear God's voice most clearly through Scripture. God alone is our protector, our defender, and the true source of all our blessings. Unfulfilled hopes often prompt us to doubt God's work in our lives. But God is always moving, even when we doubt.

How do we engage God with the concerns and anxieties of our life?

Following the above example, answer these questions.

2. How would you characterize your faith—strong and active, or shaky and passive?

3. Why do some Christians live by the principles of strict religious legalism? How do you compare that sort of lifestyle with Abraham's faith in God?

4. When we say that we have a covenant relationship with God, what does that mean?

5. How do you view yourself and your relationship with God in light of the covenant-making ritual described in this story?

6. Based on God's words in this story about the Egyptians and the Canaanites, what can we infer about the way God works in the nations of our world today?

7. What are God's eternal and covenantal promises to those who put their faith in him through Jesus Christ?

Invitation and Response

God's Word always invites a response. Think about the way the story of God's covenant with Abraham speaks to us today. How does the story invite us to respond?

God is
always
moving,
even when
we doubt.

GENESIS 21:1–21

This story is somewhat similar to the Sarah-Abraham-Hagar story in chapter 16: both narratives contain family conflict, the threat of death in the wilderness, and God rescuing those in danger. However, there are also important differences: while chapter 16 focuses on the rights of Abraham's two wives, this story focuses on the inheritance rights of Abraham's two sons. Abraham plays a passive role in chapter 16 (in verse 6 he tells Sarah, "Do . . . whatever you think best"); in chapter 21, when Sarah demands that Abraham banish Hagar and Ishmael, Abraham is anguished about Ishmael's fate (verses 10–11). In chapter 16, Hagar runs away because Sarah is mistreating her; in chapter 21, Abraham expels her and Ishmael from the house. In chapter 16, God does not speak to Abraham; in chapter 21, he does. Finally, chapter 21 devotes more attention to Ishmael than it does to Isaac and elevates him as a significant character in Abraham's story; though he stands outside the covenant faith, he is also Abraham's son and enjoys God's presence.

WEEK 4, DAY 1

Listen to the story in Genesis 21:1–21 by reading it aloud several times until you become familiar with its verses, words, and phrases. Enjoy the experience of imagining the story in your mind, picturing each event as it unfolds.

WEEK 4 DAY 2

The Setting

The immediate context for this story, of course, is God's promise to Abraham that Sarah would give birth to a son (18:10–15; see also 17:15–19). Isaac's birth heralds the beginning of the fulfillment of the promises God made to Abraham at various times, beginning with their first encounter (12:2; 13:16; 15:4–5; 17:5–6). God's command to keep his covenant (17:9–14) sets the stage for Isaac's circumcision when he is eight days old (21:4). The story of Ishmael in 21:8–21 is a continuation of Hagar's story from chapter 16.

Stories of Abraham and Abimelek precede (Genesis 20) and follow (21:22–34) the story of Abraham's family (21:1–21), and though the conflict between Abraham and Abimelek is resolved, the conflict within Abraham's own household continues. In addition, the report of Isaac's birth (21:1–7) is directly linked to the healing of the barren women in Abimelek's household (20:17–18)—the women's infertility and subsequent healing anticipate Sarah's healing and the birth of the son God promised her. Thus, God's creation blessing—"be fruitful and increase in number" (Genesis 1:28)—is at work in both the covenant family and in Abimelek's family.

The story of Abraham and Ishmael in 21:8–21 is also connected to the story of chapter 22; in 21:14, Abraham sends Ishmael into the wilderness, and in 22:3, he takes Isaac to a mountain with the intent of offering him as a sacrifice. Both sons are faced with the possibility of death; however, both live when God intervenes to save them (21:17–21; 22:11–14).

The Plot

Now let's look carefully at how the writer organizes the stories of 21:1–21—the plot will become clear as we examine the various parts of this story. Based on the transitions we notice in these verses, we can divide 21:1–21 into seven smaller paragraphs of verses. Let's examine each of those seven paragraphs one at a time. **Beneath each grouping of verses, write the primary idea or theme they communicate (follow the pattern provided for 21:1–5, 6–7, and 8–10).**

1. Genesis 21:1–5

God graciously fulfills the promise he made to Sarah and Abraham—she gives birth to a son, and Abraham names him Isaac.

2. Genesis 21:6–7

Sarah acknowledges God for bringing gladness into her life and enabling her to bear Abraham a son in his old age.

3. Genesis 21:8–10

Sarah demands that Abraham expel Hagar and Ishmael from the household and thus secure Isaac's future as the sole heir.

4. Genesis 21:11–13

5. Genesis 21:14

6. Genesis 21:15–18

7. Genesis 21:19–21

WEEK 4, DAY 3

What's Happening in the Story?

As we notice certain circumstances in the story, we will begin to see how they are similar to or different from the realities of our world. The story will become the lens through which we see the world in which we live today. In our study today, you may encounter words and/or phrases that are unfamiliar to you. Some of the particular words and translation choices for them have been explained in more detail in the **Word Study Notes**. If you are interested in even more help or detail, you can supplement this study with a Bible dictionary or other Bible study resource.

1. Genesis 21:1–5

These verses show God faithfully fulfilling the promise made to Abraham and Sarah (see Genesis 17:16; 18:10) at the time specified—Abraham is one hundred years old when Sarah gives birth to a son.[1] These verses also show Abraham's faithful obedience to God's instructions; he names his son Isaac and circumcises him on the eighth day of his life.[2]

WORD STUDY NOTES #1

[1] "The LORD was gracious to Sarah" is literally translated "the LORD visited [*paqad*] Sarah." In general, this phrase refers to God's direct intervention in human affairs, either to bless or to curse. In Psalm 8:4, the same Hebrew verb, translated in the NIV as "care," conveys the LORD's concern for humans. The Old Testament also uses this verb to convey God's judgment (see Exodus 20:5, where it is translated "punishing").

[2] God provided Isaac's name (*yitzhaq*) in Genesis 17:19. The name means "he [God] laughs." Both Abraham and Sarah laughed in disbelief when God promised them a son (see 17:17 and 18:12), but now their son's name would remind them that God had the last laugh. In accordance with God's command, Isaac is the first infant the Old Testament recorded as having undergone circumcision on the eighth day (see 17:12).

2. Genesis 21:6–7

These verses show Sarah laughing again—this time, not in disbelief at God's promise but in amazement at its fulfillment. She is confident that all who hear the report of God's faithfulness will rejoice with her. She is surprised by the miracle of her motherhood and her ability to give Abraham a son in his old age.

3. Genesis 21:8–10

In these verses we see the joy and celebration in Abraham's house turning to fear, anxiety, and hostility. The festivities for Isaac's weaning[1] suddenly end when Sarah sees Ishmael, Hagar's[2] son, mocking[3] Isaac. She demands that Abraham expel Hagar and her son from the house—she refuses to let

WORD STUDY NOTES #3

[1] This celebration most likely took place when Isaac was three years old—the customary age to stop breastfeeding a child in the ancient Near East.

[2] The text probably calls Hagar "the Egyptian" not only to describe her ethnic identity but also to convey her position as an outsider to the covenant family.

Ishmael share in Abraham's wealth. As far as she is concerned, the inheritance rights belong solely to Isaac.

Practice the above pattern to write a short summary of the world or reality portrayed in the following sections:

4. Genesis 21:11–13[1, 2]

5. Genesis 21:14[1, 2]

[3] The Hebrew verb translated "mocking" here can have positive or negative connotations. In previous instances, the verb conveys laughter (17:17–19; 18:12–13). In 19:14, it means "joking." The NIV translation reflects the historical Christian and Jewish interpretation—that Sarah responds harshly to Ishmael because he mistreats Isaac (see Galatians 4:29, where Paul uses the word "persecuted" to describe Ishmael's actions). Most contemporary Christian and Jewish interpreters now use the verb's usual translation and believe that Ishmael is amusing himself or simply playing with Isaac (see "playing" in the NRSV).

WORD STUDY NOTES #4

[1] Note that the narrator describes Ishmael as "his [Abraham's] son." We can safely assume that Abraham is distressed because he loves his firstborn son.

[2] Though God sides with Sarah and tells Abraham to listen to her, God focuses in his speech on who will be the heir to his covenant with Abraham (21:12–13; see 17:19–21).

WORD STUDY NOTES #5

[1] The food (bread) and water that Abraham gave Hagar would have lasted only a few days in the desert.

[2] "The Desert of Beersheba" refers to the southern part of the Negev, the southern border of Canaan.

WORD STUDY NOTES #6

[1] "The angel of God" who speaks to Hagar is God himself (see 16:7–13). The Old Testament often refers to the voice of the angel and the voice of God interchangeably.

[2] In Scripture, "Do not be afraid" is a common word of comfort and assurance to those who are anxious or in dangerous situations (see 15:1).

[3] The phrase "God has heard" is the basis of the name Ishmael (*yishmael*) (see 16:11).

6. Genesis 21:15–18[1, 2, 3]

WORD STUDY NOTES #7

[1] Ishmael's skill as an archer suggests his lifestyle as a hunter and warrior in the desert.

[2] "Paran" is a general designation for the wilderness of the eastern Sinai Peninsula, an area that stretches to the Red Sea in the south and Kadesh in the north. This may have been where Ishmael's descendants lived.

7. Genesis 21:19–21[1, 2]

Discoveries

Let's summarize some of our discoveries from Genesis 21:1–21.

1. God fulfilled his promise by giving Abraham and Sarah a son.
2. Abraham obeyed God's instructions by naming his son Isaac and circumcising him when he was eight days old.

3. Sarah acknowledged God as the source of her joy and laughter.
4. Sarah's rejoicing ended when she saw her son and Ishmael together; she wanted Isaac to be the sole heir to the family's inheritance.
5. God urged Abraham to listen to Sarah's demands but recognized both Isaac and Ishmael as Abraham's offspring.
6. Abraham sent Hagar and Ishmael away from his house and into the wilderness.
7. When their water ran out, Hagar prayed she would not have to see her son die in the wilderness.
8. God heard Ishmael's cry and spoke words of comfort and assurance to Hagar.
9. God provided water for them and promised Hagar that he would make Ishmael into a great nation.

WEEK 4, DAY 4

The Isaac-Ishmael Story and the Story of God

The most extensive New Testament reference to the story of Abraham, Sarah, Isaac, Hagar, and Ishmael is found in Galatians 4:21–31. Paul uses his interpretation of this story to support his argument that those who are in Christ are free from the law. He begins by contrasting Abraham's two sons—one born by a slave woman, according to the flesh, and the other born by a free woman, according to God's promise. Paul views the two women as representative of two covenants: Hagar represents the covenant made at Mount Sinai, in which children are born into slavery (to the law). Paul also links Mount Sinai to the earthly city of Jerusalem, a city in bondage to the law. Conversely, those who are free from the law are the children of the heavenly Jerusalem—like Isaac, they are children of promise. Paul interprets Ishmael's interaction with Isaac in Genesis 21:9 as persecution, and relates it to the way that those who insist on keeping the Jewish law persecute those who claim freedom from the law through Christ. Paul concludes by exhorting his readers to claim their inheritance in Christ by distancing themselves from those who are in bondage to the law: "Get rid of the slave woman and her son, for the slave woman's son will never share in the inheritance with the free woman's son" (4:30). With this story, Paul demonstrates for the early Christians how to read Old Testament scriptures in light of Christ's new covenant. **In the space given below, write a short summary of how the following passages are related to the various aspects of the story of Genesis 21:1-21:**

1. Genesis 16:10; 17:20

2. Genesis 16:15

3. Genesis 17:16

4. Genesis 17:17

5. Genesis 17:21; 18:10

6. Genesis 18:13

7. Acts 7:8

8. Romans 7:6–8

9. Hebrews 11:17–18

WEEK 4, DAY 5

Genesis and Our World Today

When we enter into the intriguing narrative of Genesis 21:1-21, the story becomes the lens through which we see ourselves, our world, and God's action in our world today.

1. What does this Genesis story say to us about ourselves, our world, and God's action in our world today?

we experience God's faithfulness to us in various ways, most importantly in the fulfillment of his promise of salvation to us through his Son, Jesus Christ. obedience to God's instructions and commands through our actions is the most appropriate way to respond to God's faithfulness we enjoy in our life. We are like Sarah in many ways in that though we rejoice in what God does for us, we are often reluctant to share God's blessings with others around us. Outsiders are seldom welcomed by most people in our world and they tend to keep them away.

Describe what privileged and powerful people do to protect and safeguard their future at the expense of the powerless and the vulnerable in our world.

2. How does Abraham's agony at sending Hagar and Ishmael away compare with our attitudes about refugees and undocumented immigrants (some of whom are, like Ishmael, children with nowhere to go and no hope for the future)?

3. What does God's speech to Abraham in 21:12–13 tell us about the way God works to fulfill God's plans in our imperfect world?

4. How do the scenes in verses 14–16 compare with the despair and hopelessness we see in refugee camps and impoverished areas of the world?

5. What do verses 17–20 tell us about the way God works in the lives of exiled and forsaken people?

Invitation and Response

God's Word always invites a response. Think about the way the story of Isaac and Ishmael speaks to us today. How does the story invite us to respond?

Though Ishmael stands outside the covenant faith, he is also Abraham's son and enjoys God's presence.

GENESIS 22:1–19

In the Jewish tradition, this narrative is popularly known as *Akedah* ("the binding") because of Abraham's binding of Isaac in verse 9. As we'll see later, this story is closely related to the story of Ishmael in 21:8–21. It also bears some similarities to the story of God's initial encounter with Abraham (12:1–3). In both stories, God commands Abraham to "go" (12:1; 22:2). In 12:1, God commands Abraham to renounce his past, his family roots, and his relationships ("your country, your people, and your father's household") and go to the land God will show him. In 22:2, God commands him to give up the future wrapped up in his beloved son ("Take your son, your only son, whom you love"), and go to offer him as a burnt offering on a mountain God would show him. In this story, we see Abraham's awareness of God's sovereign lordship over his life; Abraham obeys God's command even though it appears to mean giving up the future God promised him.

This narrative foreshadows the Jewish law stipulating God's claim on firstborn sons and his provision for their redemption (see Exodus 22:29; 34:20)—we see this provision for redemption on display as God commands Abraham to sacrifice his only son yet provides a ram instead (22:2, 13). Additionally, while neighboring people groups commonly practiced child sacrifice (and, at times, so did Israel), this narrative makes the strongest case in the Old Testament against such practices (see Leviticus 20:2–5; 2 Kings 3:27; Jeremiah 7:31).

WEEK 5, DAY 1

Listen to the story in Genesis 22:1–19 by reading it aloud several times until you become familiar with its verses, words, and phrases. Enjoy the experience of imagining the story in your mind, picturing each event as it unfolds.

WEEK 5, DAY 2

The Setting

This story constitutes the climax of the encounters between God and Abraham in Genesis 12–25. God's promise of descendants (12:2), his promise to give Sarah a son and Abraham an heir to the covenant (17:19), and the birth of Isaac (21:1–5) form the context for this story. Though the chapter's opening phrase, "some time later" (22:1), does not specify how much time has elapsed since the stories of chapter 21, we see that Isaac is old enough to carry the wood for the offering and to question his father about the lamb (see verse 6).

The writer may have placed this story after the story of Ishmael (21:8–21) to highlight the uncanny parallels between the narratives. In chapter 21, Sarah demands that Abraham send Ishmael away; in chapter 22, God demands that Abraham send Isaac away. In both stories, Abraham obeys God's command and rises "early the next morning" (21:14; 22:3). One son he sends into the wilderness to probable death; the other he takes on a journey to offer him as a sacrifice. In both stories, the angel of God/the LORD speaks from heaven. In chapter 21, God opens Hagar's eyes so she sees a well of water; in chapter 22, Abraham looks up and sees a ram. God intervenes and spares the lives of both sons, providing water for Ishmael and a ram to be sacrificed in place of Isaac. In both stories, God makes promises to Abraham about his sons' futures (21:13; 22:17–18). Together, these two narratives form the tale of Abraham's two sons: Ishmael the outsider and Isaac the insider. These literary parallels also highlight the importance of both stories to the larger story of God and Abraham in Genesis.

The Plot

Now let's look carefully at how the writer organizes the story of 22:1–19—the plot will become clear as we examine the various parts of this story. Based on the transitions we notice in these verses, we can divide 22:1–19 into six smaller paragraphs. Let's examine each of those six paragraphs one at a time. **Beneath each grouping of verses, write the primary idea or theme they communicate (follow the pattern provided for 22:1–2, 3–5, and 6–8).**

1. Genesis 22:1–2

God commands Abraham to offer Isaac as a burnt offering on a mountain in the region of Moriah.

2. Genesis 22:3–5

Abraham sets out for the mountain with his servants and his son, and then leaves the servants behind on the third day of the journey.

3. Genesis 22:6–8

Abraham and Isaac continue the journey, and Abraham tells Isaac that God will provide the lamb for the offering.

4. Genesis 22:9–12

5. Genesis 22:13-14

6. Genesis 22:15–19

WEEK 5, DAY 3

What's Happening in the Story?

As we notice certain circumstances in the story, we will begin to see how they are similar to or different from the realities of our world. The story will become the lens through which we see the world in which we live today. In our study today, you may encounter words and/or phrases that are unfamiliar to you. Some of the particular words and translation choices for them have been explained in more detail in the **Word Study Notes**. If you are interested in even more help or detail, you can supplement this study with a Bible dictionary or other Bible study resource.

1. Genesis 22:1–2

The narrator introduces God's demand as a test so that the readers/listeners of the story know something at the beginning that Abraham does not. Abraham responds to God with attentiveness and readiness to obey what God asks him to do.[1] God asks Abraham to offer Isaac, his beloved son,[2] as a burnt offering[3] on a mountain in the region of Moriah, and promises to direct Abraham to the specific location of the sacrifice.

2. Genesis 22:3–5

Abraham obeys God's command without raising objections or asking questions.[1] After gathering the wood needed for the offering, Abraham sets out with Isaac and two servants to fulfill God's command.[2] On the third day,[3] Abraham recognizes the offering site in the distance and asks the servants to stay behind while he and Isaac continue their journey. He tells the servants that they will return after worshiping God at the designated place.[4]

3. Genesis 22:6–8

Abraham and Isaac continue their journey with Isaac carrying the wood and Abraham carrying the fire and the knife. Isaac, unaware of his father's plan, breaks the silence with a penetrat-

WORD STUDY NOTES #1

[1] In the Old Testament, the phrase "here am I" appears in multiple places to indicate the readiness of the person addressed to obey the command given.

[2] The terms God uses to describe Isaac—"your son, your only son, whom you love"—are expressions of endearment that progress from the general to the intimate. With these words, God acknowledges the deep pain this command will cause Abraham should he choose to obey.

[3] In the Old Testament sacrificial system, making a burnt offering is an act of worship. According to Leviticus 1:3–17, a burnt offering is to be completely consumed by the fire on the altar. This practice shows a worshiper's total dedication to God.

WORD STUDY NOTES #2

[1] The fact that Abraham did not object to God's command suggests that he is aware of human sacrifice as a form of worship—his kin in Haran and Ur may have even practiced it. Though God commanded the Israelites to offer him their firstborn sons (meaning livestock), God specifically prohibited child sacrifice (see Exodus 34:19–20; Leviticus 18:21; Leviticus 20:1–6). The narrator's introduction of this story as a test prevents us from concluding that God required human sacrifice in Abraham's day.

ing question.[1] Abraham replies that God himself will provide the lamb,[2] and the two continue on their journey together.[3]

Practice the above pattern to write a short summary of the reality portrayed in the following sections:

4. Genesis 22:9–12[1, 2]

5. Genesis 22:13–14[1, 2, 3]

[2] Lack of any reference to Sarah led some early Jewish scholars to conclude that Abraham concealed the true purpose of this journey from her for fear of her opposition.

[3] In the Old Testament, three days is designated as the length of time needed to prepare for important events (see Genesis 31:22; Exodus 3:18; 5:3; Numbers 10:33; Jonah 3:3; Esther 5:1). It would have taken the group three days to make the forty-mile journey by foot.

[4] Abraham's words "we will come back to you" reveal his confidence that God will intervene and save Isaac's life (see verse 8).

WORD STUDY NOTES #3

[1] Isaac's question is logical—it was the responsibility of the worshiper to bring the animal for sacrifice.

[2] Abraham's reply displays his confidence that if he is to carry out God's command and God is to keep his promises, there must be another provision for the sacrifice.

[3] The phrase "went on together" (verses 6, 8) conveys the intimacy of Abraham and Isaac's relationship and their bond as father and son.

6. Genesis 22:15–19[1, 2]

Discoveries

Let's summarize our discoveries from Genesis 22:1–19.

1. God tested Abraham by commanding him to offer Isaac as a burnt offering.
2. Abraham obeyed God and set out to obey his command without complaint, protest, or question.
3. On the way to the mountain, when Isaac questioned his father about the animal for the sacrifice, Abraham told him that God would provide the lamb, thus displaying his trust in God's provision.
4. When he arrived at the place God showed him, Abraham built an altar, bound Isaac, and prepared to carry out the sacrifice.
5. God intervened to stop Abraham from sacrificing Isaac, indicating that this had been a test of whether Abraham would demonstrate his fear of God through action.
6. Abraham fulfilled God's demand for a burnt offering by sacrificing the ram God provided for him.

WORD STUDY NOTES #4

[1] Verse 9 marks the only occurrence of the verb "bind" (*aqad* in Hebrew) in the Old Testament. In post-biblical literature, it is used as a technical term for tying an animal's feet together.

[2] "Now I know that you fear God" reveals the purpose of Abraham's test. "Fear of God" is one's reverence and respect for God's authority over creation. This phrase does not mean that God did not know that Abraham feared God. Throughout the story of Abraham, he is presented as a man who held deep reverence for God as the Creator of heaven and earth (see 14:22–23). The nature and quality of Abraham's fear of God is being tested. Would Abraham demonstrate his fear of God through unreserved obedience?

WORD STUDY NOTES #5

[1] "The LORD will provide" or "the LORD provides" (*Yahweh-yireh*) could also be translated "the LORD sees."

[2] "On the mountain of the LORD it will be provided" could also be translated "in the mountain of the LORD he shall be seen," which conveys the idea of God making himself visible through action.

[3] The provision of the ram shows that, though God initiated the test, God also resolved it. In that sense, this story is about God, and Abraham is just the primary human character.

WORD STUDY NOTES #6

[1] The promises God makes here are reiterations of previous promises, with the exception of the promise that Abraham's descendants will take possession of their enemies' cities.

[2] The lack of reference to Isaac in verse 19 parallels the absence of Sarah at the beginning of this story. Perhaps Isaac was intentionally omitted at the end to show that the story was actually about God.

7. As a reward for Abraham's obedience, God promised to bless him, give him numerous descendants, and bless the nations on earth through them.
8. This entire story is a story about God in which Abraham is merely the primary human character.

WEEK 5, DAY 4

The Story of God Testing Abraham and the Story of God

Though the *Akedah* story represents the most critical event in Abraham's life, it is not mentioned again in the Old Testament. However, two New Testament writers offer different but complementary interpretations of this story. The author of Hebrews interprets the story as an example of Abraham's triumphant faith in God's commitment to fulfill his promises. In the author's view, "Abraham reasoned that God could even raise the dead, and so in a manner of speaking he did receive Isaac back from death" (Hebrews 11:17–19). In his epistle, James cites this story as evidence for his assertion that "faith without deeds is useless," and argues that Abraham was "considered righteous for what he did when he offered his son Isaac on the altar." James goes on to argue that faith and actions work together (James 2:20–24).

In addition to these two passages, we find other scriptures that directly relate to different aspects of this story. **In the space provided below, write a short summary of how each passage relates to the various aspects of the story of Genesis 22:1–19:**

1. Genesis 12:3; Acts 3:25; Galatians 3:8

____

____

____

____

____

2. Genesis 15:5; 26:4; 32:12

____

____

____

____

3. Genesis 21:17

____

____

____

____

4. Genesis 24:60

5. Genesis 26:5

6. Isaiah 45:23; Jeremiah 22:5; Amos 6:8

7. Hebrews 6:13–14

WEEK 5, DAY 5

Genesis and Our World Today

When we enter into the intriguing narrative of Genesis 22:1-19, the story becomes the lens through which we see ourselves, our world, and God's action in our world today. Though the realities portrayed in this story have no known parallels in the story of the Bible, the listening community can see in it reflections of themselves and their own struggles to keep faith in the midst of extremely painful challenges they face in their lives.

1. What does this Genesis story say to us about ourselves, our world, and God's action in our world today?

we often chafe at the thought of giving up the things we value, even for our relationship with God. We also often view our troubles as a test of our faith, though sometimes they may be the outcome of our own unwise decisions. The story portrays Abraham's attentiveness to God and readiness to obey.

Describe attentiveness to God in your life and in the church world in general.

2. How do we show our obedience to God during critical times in our lives?

3. How confident are we when we express our faith?

4. What does "fear of God" mean today? How does it compare with Abraham's fear of God?

5. Abraham's obedience was not motivated by thought of any reward from God. How does this compare with our motivation when we obey God?

6. What does this story say about the manner in which God demonstrates his trustworthiness to us?

7. What does this story say about the larger purpose of God's testing that we may experience in our lives?

Invitation and Response

God's Word always invites a response. Think about the way the story of God testing Abraham speaks to us today. How does the story invite us to respond?

Abraham obeys God's command even though it appears to mean giving up the future God promised him.

GENESIS 26:1-33

This is the only story in Genesis that focuses primarily on Isaac's life and activities. In other stories, he lives in the shadow of his famous father or his infamous son. In presenting his wife as his sister (26:7–11), Isaac parallels Abraham's deception in 12:10–20 and 20:1–18. However, there are also significant differences between Abraham and Isaac's stories.

While God allows Abraham to go to Egypt during the famine in Canaan (12:10–20), he forbids Isaac from doing the same (26:2). While Pharaoh takes Sarah as his wife, the ruler of Gerar does not take Rebekah. God intervenes in Abraham and Sarah's case, but the king of Gerar discovers the truth about Isaac and Rebekah by his own observation, and Isaac does not get rich from his scheme. Abimelek's treaty with Isaac (26:26–31) parallels the treaty he made with Abraham (21:22–34); both agreements center on peaceful relations between the Philistines and the sojourning patriarchs. A unique feature of this narrative is that God speaks to Isaac twice and reaffirms his covenant promises (26:3–4, 24).

Most likely, the encounter between Abraham and Abimelek (chapter 20) takes place before Isaac's birth, while Isaac and Abimelek's encounter (chapter 26) occurs after Abraham's death at the age of 175. This means there is at least a seventy-five-year gap between the two stories. Though the land of Gerar and the Philistines in this narrative may be the same ones referenced in chapters 20 and 21, we do not know the exact identity of the king or the army commander in Isaac's story. Some scholars think Abimelek and Phicol are royal names or titles rather than personal names. If this is true, these stories may feature different kings and army commanders.

WEEK 6, DAY 1

Listen to the story in Genesis 26:1–33 by reading it aloud several times until you become familiar with its verses, words, and phrases. Enjoy the experience of imagining the story in your mind, picturing each event as it unfolds.

WEEK 6, DAY 2

The Setting

This is the first time in Genesis where we see God transferring the promises made to Abraham directly to Isaac. Though Abraham received God's promises and designated Isaac to be heir to the covenant, we have no record of Abraham informing Isaac of this. We would expect Abraham to bestow his blessings—including God's promises (see Isaac's blessing of Jacob in 28:3–4)—upon Isaac before Abraham's death. However, Isaac receives the promises from God after Abraham's death and burial (25:7–11).

The lack of reference to Isaac's sons here may imply that the events of chapter 26 occurred before their birth. Chapter 25 reports Jacob and Esau's birth, as well as the sale of Esau's birthright; the nature of that transaction suggests that the brothers were at least adolescents at that point, if not older. The fact that this story appears after the account of Jacob and Esau's birth demonstrates how the events of Genesis are not always arranged in precise chronological order. Even if Jacob and Esau were born before the events of chapter 26, they would have been small children at this point.

A famine in Canaan is the immediate setting of this story. Isaac is most likely living near Beer Lahai Roi, in the Negev region, south of Canaan (see 25:11) or Beersheba, where his father previously lived (22:19). Canaan often experienced famines due to severe drought, destruction of crops by locusts, and other natural calamities; during these times, people survived by going to Egypt for their food supply (see Abraham's story in 12:10–20).

This story is set in the larger theological context of God's encounter with Abraham, his promises to Abraham, and Abraham's God-given mission to be a blessing to all peoples on earth (12:3). In this story, God gives Isaac the same promises and mission.

The Plot

Now let's look carefully at how the writer organizes the story of 26:1–33—the plot will become clear as we examine the various parts of this story. Based on the transitions we notice in these verses, we can divide 26:1–33 into six smaller paragraphs. Let's examine each of those six paragraphs one at a time. **Beneath each grouping of verses, write the primary idea or theme they communicate (follow the pattern provided for 26:1–6, 7–11, and 12–15).**

1. Genesis 26:1-6

God appears to Isaac during a famine in Canaan and tells him to stay in Gerar rather than go to Egypt. God promises to be with Isaac and confers on him the promises he made to Abraham.

2. Genesis 26:7–11

Isaac lies about his relationship with Rebekah, but the king discovers the truth. When the king questions him, Isaac admits that he was afraid he would be killed on his wife's account. The king responds by ordering the death penalty for anyone who harms Isaac or Rebekah.

3. Genesis 26:12–15

God blesses Isaac with flocks, herds, and a plentiful harvest. The Philistines become jealous of Isaac's prosperity and cut off his access to water.

4. Genesis 26:16–22

5. Genesis 26:23–25

6. Genesis 26:26–33

WEEK 6, DAY 3

What's Happening in the Story?

As we notice certain circumstances in the story, we will begin to see how they are similar to or different from the realities of our world. The story will become the lens through which we see the world in which we live today. In our study today, you may encounter words and/or phrases that are unfamiliar to you. Some of the particular words and translation choices for them have been explained in more detail in the **Word Study Notes**. If you are interested in even more help or detail, you can supplement this study with a Bible dictionary or other Bible study resource.

1. Genesis 26:1-6

A famine in Canaan prompts Isaac to travel to Gerar in the land of the Philistines. God appears to Isaac and tells him not to go to Egypt[1] but to stay in Philistine territory. God then promises to be with Isaac, bless him, make his descendants numerous as the stars in the sky, and give them the lands he promised Abraham. God also promises to bless all nations on earth through his descendants.[2] Because of Abraham's loyalty and obedience to God's commands,[3] God hands the promises he made to Abraham down to Isaac.

WORD STUDY NOTES #1

[1] Some scholars speculate that Isaac set out for Egypt because of their abundant food supply. Perhaps God did not want Isaac to have the same experiences Abraham did on his journey to Egypt.

[2] See where God made these promises to Abraham in Genesis 12:1-3; 13:15; 15:5, 18; 22:16-18.

[3] "Commands," "decrees," and "instructions" are synonyms for the Law (Torah) God gave Israel at Mount Sinai. Verse 5 describes Abraham as a role model for Torah obedience long before his descendants received the Law at Mount Sinai.

2. Genesis 26:7-11

When the men of Gerar ask Isaac about Rebekah, he tells them she is his sister. The lie is to preserve his own life; he is afraid that if he tells the truth, he will be killed on account of his wife's beauty.[1] However, the Philistine king Abimelek sees a display of intimacy between Isaac and Rebekah. When the king asks Isaac why he tried to pass off his wife as his sister, Isaac tells the truth.[2] The king rebukes Isaac for endangering his people through his deception.[3] Then the king issues a royal decree to prevent the people of Gerar from harming Isaac or Rebekah.

WORD STUDY NOTES #2

[1] See Genesis 12:11-13; 20:2, 11 for similar episodes in Abraham's story.

[2] See similar confrontations in Genesis 12:18-19 and 20:8-10.

[3] See how God punishes Pharaoh and his household in 12:17, and Abimelek's household in 20:18.

3. Genesis 26:13–15

God blesses Isaac with a tremendous harvest in the land of the Philistines, where he lives as a sojourner.[1] Thanks to God's blessings, Isaac gains status as a wealthy person with flocks, herds, and servants.[2] But the Philistines envy Isaac's good fortune. So to impede his success (and perhaps force him to leave Gerar), they fill his family's wells with dirt, denying them access to the water they need for survival.[3]

Practice the above pattern to write a short description of the reality portrayed in the following sections:

4. Genesis 26:16–22[1, 2, 3]

____

____

____

____

____

____

____

____

____

5. Genesis 26:23–25[1, 2, 3]

____

____

____

____

____

____

____

____

WORD STUDY NOTES #3

[1] Though this story tells us that Isaac plants crops, there is no indication that he follows a farming lifestyle. Isaac, like his father, Abraham, and his son Jacob, is probably a seminomadic shepherd with flocks and herds.

[2] It is important to note that, while Abraham got rich from pagan kings (see Genesis 12:16; 20:14–16), Isaac gains his wealth exclusively through God's blessing. This list of riches implies that God is blessing Isaac despite his deceptive interaction with the Philistines.

[3] In the ancient world, wells belonged to those who dug them and their families.

WORD STUDY NOTES #4

[1] Abimelek's words to Isaac—"you have become too powerful for us"—convey his fear that Isaac could jeopardize the king's power in Gerar if he continues to amass wealth.

[2] In the ancient world, naming wells was a way of claiming property rights over them.

[3] The footnotes in your Bible should explain the meanings of the names Isaac gives to his wells: Esek, Sitnah, and Rehoboth.

WORD STUDY NOTES #5

[1] The phrase "the God of your father" emphasizes the distinctive and unique relationship between

God and Abraham. The phrase is later used many times to reference both Isaac and Jacob as well as Abraham (see, for example, Genesis 28:13; 31:42, 53; Exodus 3:6).

[2] God uses the title "my servant" here and elsewhere to recognize those who are loyal and faithful to God. Moses, Caleb, and David are among the few people in the Old Testament to receive the designation (see Numbers 12:7; 14:24; 2 Samuel 7:5).

[3] By building an altar, Isaac follows the example of his father, who already made Beersheba a place of worship (Genesis 21:33).

WORD STUDY NOTES #6

[1] A "sworn agreement" is a solemn oath with a curse attached. The curse is meant to serve as a deterrent to the party who would break the treaty.

6. Genesis 26:26-33[1]

____

____

____

____

____

Discoveries

Let's summarize some of our discoveries from Genesis 26:1–33.

1. God appeared to Isaac during a famine in Canaan and told him not to go to Egypt but to remain in the Philistine town of Gerar.
2. God promised to give Isaac his presence and blessing, land, and numerous descendants as a reward for Abraham's loyalty and obedience.
3. Though Isaac lied and said Rebekah was his sister, Abimelek discovered the truth and rebuked Isaac for endangering others with his deception.
4. Isaac enjoyed God's blessings in his life and activities, and though he and Rebekah were guaranteed protection by the king, the Philistines envied his prosperity and initiated property disputes with Isaac over his family's wells.
5. When Abimelek asked Isaac to leave Gerar, Isaac did so without complaint and settled in a valley outside Gerar.
6. God appeared to Isaac in Beersheba and again promised his presence, his blessing, and an increase of descendants, to which Isaac responded by building an altar and worshiping God.
7. The Philistine king recognized Isaac as a powerful person who enjoyed God's blessings and was thus a threat, so he proposed a treaty of nonaggression.
8. Isaac reminded the king of his prior hostility but also took the initiative to establish a peaceful relationship with him by swearing an oath.

WEEK 6, DAY 4

The Isaac-Abimelek Story and the Story of God

God's promises to Isaac show how this story connects to the other stories in Genesis about Israel's ancestors. These promises also elevate Isaac to be one of the three great forefathers of Israel; throughout the story of the Bible, Isaac remains a crucial link between Abraham (the original recipient of God's covenant promises) and Jacob (whose twelve sons become the twelve tribes of Israel).

After Genesis, the story in 26:1–33 does not receive much attention elsewhere in the Bible. Paul picks up the theme of God's blessing upon all nations in Galatians 3:8 but links it to God's promise to Abraham rather than to Isaac. Still, Isaac's obedience to God, his non-confrontational response to those who treat him with hostility, and his efforts to live in peace with others are all qualities God expects to find among his people.

We have already referenced three parallels between Abraham and Isaac's stories (see 12:10–20; 20:1–18; 21:22–33). We will now look at passages that recall God's promises to Israel's ancestors, as well as passages that address the qualities Isaac displays in chapter 26.

In the space given below, write a short summary of how the following passages are related to the various aspects of the story of Genesis 26:1-33:

1. Genesis 28:13–15

____

____

____

____

____

2. Psalm 31:8

____

____

____

____

3. Psalm 37:1–2, 11

4. Psalm 37:7

5. Matthew 5:9

6. Romans 12:18

WEEK 6, DAY 5

Genesis and Our World Today

When we enter into the intriguing narrative of Genesis 26:1-33, the story becomes the lens through which we can see ourselves, our world, and God's action in our world today. Though the realities portrayed in this story belong to an ancient world, the listening community can see in it reflections of themselves and their own struggles to keep faith in the midst of extremely painful challenges they face in their lives.

1. What does this Genesis story say to us about ourselves, our world, and God's actions in our lives today?

Scarcity can motivate us to seek security through our own schemes and strategies. Just as Isaac became the heir of God's promises because of his father's loyalty and obedience, today's believers are heirs to God's promises because of the faithful legacy of those who have gone before. Isaac's fear of being killed because of his wife's beauty is a reality for modern-day families who live in refugee camps or embark on dangerous journeys in search of asylum.

2. Based on verses 11-12, what can be said about the ways God works in our world?

3. What is our usual reaction or response when other people challenge our rights and disrupt our lives?

4. How does the king's order (verse 16) bear upon our attitudes toward immigrant communities in our neighborhoods?

5. How do people today, including believers, settle their disputes?

6. What are some ways by which God works in our lives to make room for us to grow and flourish?

7. How does Isaac's approach toward peacemaking differ from modern-day approaches toward peace negotiations? (Remember that in the conflict with Abimelek's people, Isaac was both the offended and the stronger party.)

8. When we consider Isaac's peaceable conduct in this story, how does our own behavior compare?

Invitation and Response

God's Word always invites a response. Think about the way the story of Isaac and Abimelek speaks to us today. How does the story invite us to respond?

Today's believers are heirs to God's promises because of the faithful legacy of those who have gone before.

GENESIS 27:1–45

This is a family story in which the father, the mother, and their two sons all play crucial roles, and conflict over a final blessing drives the action. Some commentators see the events of this story as representative of the ancient Amorite final-blessing ceremony: the father requests a special favor from the firstborn son; the son fulfills the father's request; the father verifies that the blessing recipient is indeed the firstborn; the father kisses the firstborn and pronounces the blessing.

This story's scenes are filled with deception: with guidance from his scheming mother, the younger son deceives his old, blind father and steals the blessing intended for the firstborn. The story also shows that, once the father pronounces his blessing, he cannot take it back—the powerful words have already taken effect.

The language of this story emphasizes the importance of the final-blessing theme—the word "blessing" and its verb form ("blessed," "bless") occur more than twenty times in this story. However, it is not clear how the final blessing is related to the firstborn son's right to a double share of the inheritance. Birthright only comes up when Esau laments that Jacob has taken both his birthright and his father's blessing (27:36).

WEEK 7, DAY 1

Listen to the story in Genesis 27:1–45 by reading it aloud several times until you become familiar with its verses, words, and phrases. Enjoy the experience of imagining the story in your mind, picturing each event as it unfolds.

WEEK 7, DAY 2

The Setting

God's promise to Abraham—to bless him with numerous descendants and bless all families on earth through them—forms the larger theological context for this story. Isaac was born as the designated heir to this covenant, according to God's promise (17:19, 21)—and indeed, God himself conferred his covenant promises to Abraham on Isaac (26:3–4). In this story, we see the third generation of this family, in which the father, in anticipation of his death, seeks to bestow his blessings on the firstborn son. This ritual would give the firstborn son the privileged place in the family as the inheritor of the blessings and promises the father received from God.

In Genesis 25:21–34, Rebekah becomes pregnant; God tells her that she carries two future nations in her womb, and that the older will serve the younger; Esau is born, followed by Jacob; and Esau sells his birthright to Jacob. These events serve as the immediate setting of 27:1–45. We do not know if Rebekah told Isaac what God said about the two boys' destinies. If she did, Isaac seems to have ignored the prophecy and decided to follow the custom of blessing the firstborn son. Moreover, though Esau's marriage to two Canaanite women grieved Isaac and Rebekah (26:34–35), Isaac's love for Esau may have led him to prefer Esau over Jacob (25:28). It is worth noting that Esau's sale of his birthright plays no role in the story of 27:1–45—neither parent displays any awareness of the transaction between the sons.

Rebekah's behavior in this story may be motivated not only by her love for Jacob but also by her memory of God's word about her sons. As this story makes clear, she is doggedly determined for Jacob to receive Isaac's blessing. Rebekah probably sees Jacob as the son who will carry on the family values and traditions (unlike the wayward Esau, who has become involved with the local Canaanite population).

From a theological perspective, God's word about the older brother serving the younger shows God's gracious choice of Jacob as the heir to his covenant promises. Jacob's entry into the world as a heel-grabber (25:26), and Esau's sale of his birthright for a bowl of stew (25:29–34) reveal the two sons' personalities. In chapter 28, Isaac hands God's covenant promises down to Jacob, thus confirming his words to Rebekah.

The Plot

Now let's look carefully at how the writer organizes the story of 27:1–45—the plot will become clear as we examine the various parts of this story. Based on the transitions we notice in these verses, we can divide 27:1–45 into five smaller paragraphs.

Let's examine each of those five paragraphs one at a time. **Beneath each grouping of verses, write the primary idea or theme they communicate** (**follow the pattern provided for 27:1–4, 5–17, and 18–29**).

1. Genesis 27:1–4

Isaac, in anticipation of his death, asks Esau to hunt for game and prepare his favorite food so that he may proceed to give Esau his blessing.

2. Genesis 27:5–17

Rebekah overhears Isaac's words and devises a plan to have Jacob receive Isaac's blessing. She prepares a tasty meal, disguises Jacob, and sends him to Isaac with the food.

3. Genesis 27:18–29

Twice Jacob lies about his identity when Isaac questions him. Isaac pronounces his blessing, though he may not be fully convinced of the recipient's identity.

4. Genesis 27:30–40

5. Genesis 27:41–45

WEEK 7, DAY 3

What's Happening in the Story?

As we notice certain circumstances in the story, we will begin to see how they are similar to or different from the realities of our world. The story will become the lens through which we see the world in which we live today. In our study today, you may encounter words and/or phrases that are unfamiliar to you. Some of the particular words and translation choices for them have been explained in more detail in the **Word Study Notes**. If you are interested in even more help or detail, you can supplement this study with a Bible dictionary or other Bible study resource.

1. Genesis 27:1–4

The story opens with a scene of Isaac, who is now old, blind, and expecting to die at any time,[1] asking Esau to prepare for the ritual of his final blessing.[2] Isaac asks Esau to hunt wild game and prepare it the way he likes it. Isaac also indicates his intent to bless Esau after his meal.[3]

WORD STUDY NOTES #1

[1] Though Isaac seems to expect to die soon, he actually lives for another fifteen years or more (see Genesis 35:27–29).

[2] "My son" and "Here am I" are expressions of intimacy and close relationship.

[3] Though a father customarily bestowed his final blessing on the firstborn son, he had the freedom to bestow it upon another son (see Jacob blessing Ephraim, though Manasseh was the firstborn, in Genesis 48:1–20).

2. Genesis 27:5–17

The peaceful atmosphere of the opening scene quickly dissolves amid the deception of a scheming mother and her complicit son. When Esau leaves for his hunting trip, Rebekah schemes with Jacob about how to deceive Isaac into blessing Jacob instead of Esau. She plans to prepare a tasty meal for Jacob to take to his father. Jacob worries that, because his skin is smoother than Esau's, his father will discover the deception and curse Jacob instead of blessing him. However, Rebekah is willing to take the blame if Isaac discovers the truth.[1] Jacob obeys Rebekah's instructions, and she prepares the meat according to Isaac's tastes.[2] To make the impersonation complete, she clothes Jacob with Esau's clothes and covers his hands and neck with goatskins. She then sends Jacob to Isaac with the meal she prepared.

WORD STUDY NOTES #2

[1] "Let the curse fall on me" conveys Rebekah's readiness to be held accountable for the deception. Perhaps she is convinced of the success of her scheme because of God's word to her about the destiny of her sons.

[2] Rebekah seems to have made the goat meat taste like Esau's wild game.

3. Genesis 27:18–29

The scene transitions from one of scheming to one of deception. Jacob brings the food to his father, and when Isaac asks him to identify himself, Jacob unhesitatingly says he is Esau, his firstborn.[1] Jacob asks his father to sit up, eat his game, and bless him. When Isaac asks how he found the game so quickly, Jacob credits God in an attempt to exploit his father's religious devotion. With lingering suspicions, Isaac touches him to verify his identity. He is confused because he hears Jacob's voice but feels Esau's hairy hands. Isaac starts to bless his son but stops and asks again if it is really Esau who stands before him. Jacob lies again. The deception works, and Isaac eats the food his wife prepared. As Jacob kisses his father, Isaac catches Esau's scent on his clothes and finally gives the impersonator a blessing focused on agricultural productivity and political domination. Isaac's blessing ends with a word about others—they will be blessed or cursed according to how they treat the son he has blessed.[2]

WORD STUDY NOTES #3

[1] The question "Who is it?" suggests that Isaac has difficulty recognizing his son's voice. It is possible that Jacob attempts to mimic Esau's voice but fails to convince Isaac.

[2] This pronouncement of blessings or curses on other people echoes God's promise to Abraham in 12:3.

Follow the pattern above to write a short summary of the world in the following sections:

4. Genesis 27:30–40[1, 2, 3]

WORD STUDY NOTES #4

[1] Isaac's words, "I blessed him—and indeed he will be blessed" reflect the irrevocable nature of the blessing. In ancient thought, the words of blessings take effect the moment they are pronounced.

[2] The name Jacob means "one who deceives." Esau sees a connection between his brother's name and his actions.

[3] Note that Isaac's words to Esau in verses 39–40 are not introduced as a blessing. Isaac's words about Esau serving Jacob could be forecasting Israel's domination of Edom (Esau's descendants) during David's time, which continued for about 150 years (see 2 Samuel 8:14; 2 Kings 8:20–22).

5. Genesis 27:41–45[1]

WORD STUDY NOTES #5

[1]In the ancient world, family members waited until after their father's death to take revenge against one another (see Genesis 50:15–17). Sending a father to his grave in grief was unthinkable.

Discoveries

Let's summarize some of our discoveries from Genesis 27:1–45.

1. Isaac, in anticipation of his impending death, asked Esau, his firstborn son, to prepare him a meal of wild game and receive his blessing.
2. Rebekah schemed with Jacob to have Jacob receive Isaac's blessing instead.
3. Jacob impersonated Esau and served Isaac a meal Rebekah had prepared.
4. After several attempts to confirm it was Esau who stood before him, Isaac pronounced a blessing of agricultural productivity and political domination on Jacob.
5. When Esau discovered that Jacob had stolen his blessing, he was bitter and resolved to kill Jacob once their father died.
6. Fearing Esau's revenge, Rebekah told Jacob to go to her brother Laban in Haran.

WEEK 7, DAY 4

The Jacob-Esau Story and the Story of God

Though this story is well known in the Judeo-Christian tradition, it is not referenced elsewhere in the Bible, except for a negative evaluation of Esau in Hebrews 12:16–17. The writer of Hebrews cautions his readers not to be "godless" or irreligious like Esau, who sold his inheritance rights for a single meal—though he later sought his father's blessing with tears, he did not get a second chance. Hebrews does not reference the way Jacob (with Rebekah's help) gained Isaac's blessing through deceit. Neither does the text acknowledge that God chose Jacob over his elder brother. When we read Hebrews 12:16–17 in context, it becomes clear that the writer seeks to warn his readers against forfeiting God's grace, and of the irreversibility of apostasy.

The characters' actions in this family conflict recall the stories of Cain and Abel (Genesis 4:1–16), Laban and Jacob (Genesis 29–31), and Joseph and his brothers (Genesis 37), all of which illustrate the tragic effects of strife on brotherly relationships. In this story, Jacob's behavior starkly contrasts with his grandfather's conduct in Genesis 13 (where Abraham willingly gives up his rights to make peace with his nephew Lot).

While he succeeds in his scheme against Esau, later stories show that Jacob himself falls prey to deception—first from his uncle Laban (29:1–30), then from his own sons (37:12–35). Deception becomes a way of life for his family (see his sons' massacre of the Shechemites in chapter 34 and the story of Judah and Tamar in chapter 38). Though God chose Jacob as the heir to the covenant promises, his life seems to have been a testimony to the principle "you reap what you sow" (see the stories of Jacob's continuing grief over Joseph in chapters 42–45 until they are reunited in Egypt).

Though this story does not reference God's word to Rebekah—that the older son will serve the younger (25:23)—it is central to the plot. Some commentators assert that God somehow dictated Rebekah and Jacob's deception in order to fulfill his predetermined plan for Jacob. In doing so, however, they fail to distinguish that God does not will evil or deception but works in the midst of human sin to fulfill his larger purposes in the world (see Joseph's words to his brothers in 50:20: "You intended to harm me, but God intended it for good to accomplish what is now being done, the saving of many lives"). The continuation of Jacob's story in chapter 28 shows that, though he gained his father's blessing by deceit, God confirms him as the chosen heir to the covenant promises (28:13–15).

It is important to note that Esau and Jacob are reconciled after Jacob returns to Canaan from Haran (see the heartwarming story in Genesis 33). However, their conflict later resurfaces between their descendants (Israel and Edom). Additionally, the Edomites' hatred for Israel makes them an object of frequent prophetic condemnation in the Old Testament.

We will now look at some biblical passages that address the historical conflict between Israel and Edom.

In the space given below, write a short summary of how the following passages are related to various aspects of the Jacob-Esau story in Genesis 27:1–45:

1. Numbers 20:21

2. 2 Samuel 8:13–14

3. 2 Kings 8:20–22

4. Jeremiah 49:7–22

5. Amos 1:11–12

6. Amos 9:11–12

7. Obadiah 1:1–9

8. Malachi 1:1–5

WEEK 7, DAY 5

Genesis and Our World Today

When we enter into the intriguing narrative of Genesis 27:1-45, the story becomes the lens through which we see ourselves, our world, and God's action in our world today. Though much of the realities portrayed in this story belong to the patriarchal world of God's promises, and the customs and culture of that ancient world, the listening community can see in it reflections of themselves and their actions that contribute to conflict and irreversible damage to their relationship with others.

1. What does this Genesis story say to us about ourselves, our world, and God's actions in our lives today?

We live in a world where some parents give their children preferential treatment (whether openly or privately), and where people manipulate and exploit the elderly. Deception takes place at all levels of society. After God told Rebekah that he had chosen to give her younger son prominence in the family, she decided to take matters into her own hands. Believers are prone to repeat Rebekah's mistake by commandeering the situations around them while claiming to follow God's direction for their lives.

In what areas of modern life do we see people living by the philosophy, "win at any cost"?

2. Jacob not only lied to his father but also gave credit to God for providing the game. How do people use God's name for self-serving purposes today?

3. Though God is clearly active in this story, he is referenced only indirectly by the human characters (see verses 7, 20, 28). What does that say about God's work in our lives and in our deceitful world?

4. We see bitterness, anger, and hatred in Esau's plan to kill Jacob. In what ways do we see the people around us displaying those reactions when they are deceived (particularly when deceived by loved ones)?

Invitation and Response

God's Word always invites a response. Think about the way the story of Jacob stealing Esau's blessing speaks to us today. How does the story invite us to respond?

Deception becomes a way of life. Jacob's life is a testimony to the principle "you reap what you sow."